Contents

Any words appearing in bold, **like this**, are explained in the Glossary.

Japan

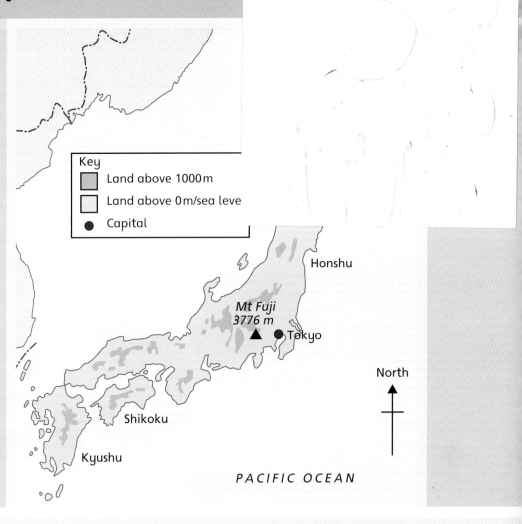

Key

Land above 1000m

Land above 0m/sea leve

● Capital

Honshu

Mt Fuji
3776 m

▲ ● Tokyo

North

Shikoku

Kyushu

PACIFIC OCEAN

Japan is an island country in Asia.
The Japanese call their country Nippon,
which means "Land of the Rising Sun".

There are 4000 islands in Japan. Most people live on the four biggest islands. They are Hokkaido, Honshu, Shikoku, and Kyushu.

Japan has many mountains and **volcanoes**. Some of the volcanoes **erupt**. Also, Japan has about 1500 **earthquakes** each year.

Japan stretches out for a long way. The north islands can have snow while the south islands are still warm. All of the islands have stormy winds called typhoons.

Many of the islands in Japan are quite small.

Landmarks

Mount Fuji is Japan's most famous mountain. It is a **volcano**. It has not **erupted** for hundreds of years.

Tokyo is the **capital**. It is Japan's largest city. One person out of every ten Japanese people lives in Tokyo.

Homes

Most people live in small flats in crowded cities. Most of the cities are on the lowlands near the coast.

In the country, there are homes made of wood. They are only one or two storeys high. Japanese people always take their shoes off when they enter a home.

Food

The Japanese enjoy making their food look attractive. They eat small portions of many different types of food but noodles are a favourite fast food.

At home, many Japanese people sit on the floor and eat from low wooden tables. They use **chopsticks** for all their food. Rice and hot tea are served at every meal.

Clothes

Farmers in the country wear **traditional** work clothes, such as baggy trousers and straw hats. Most Japanese people in the cities wear modern clothes.

Japanese people wear kimonos on special days.

Kimonos are long silk robes which are tied with a large sash. There is a different kimono for each season. The light, summer ones are called *yukata*.

Work

Only a few Japanese are farmers but they grow most of Japan's food. They grow rice, wheat, soybeans, tea, fruit, and vegetables. They also keep pigs and chickens.

16

Japan's fishermen are very successful.
They catch more fish than almost anyone
else in the world. Most people in Japan
work in offices or factories.

Transport

The bullet train is the fastest way to travel on land. There is a rail link between two of the islands through the world's longest tunnel.

The bullet train travels at a speed of 270 kilometres (170 miles) per hour.

So many people travel to work by train or **subway** that passengers are pushed onto them by station workers. Airports and motorways link all the main cities.

Language

When Japanese people greet each other, they bow to show **respect**. They speak very politely to each other.

It takes a long time to learn to read
and write Japanese. There are 1850
characters which are written in columns
from right to left.

School

Children go to school from the age of 6 to 15. They learn lots of different subjects. All Japanese children learn English. They also practise **earthquake drills**.

Most primary school children do not wear a uniform.

Most school children study very hard. Each night they do hours of homework and extra lessons. They work hard to get into a good college.

Sumo wrestling is Japan's national sport. Each wrestler has to throw the other one out of the ring. Millions of Japanese also enjoy baseball.

Many Japanese regularly visit parks
and gardens. A favourite time to go
is in the spring when the cherry trees
are in blossom.

This park is in a new
city called Ina.

Celebrations

Japan has many festivals but New Year is the biggest. People eat special food and send each other New Year's cards.

The kites on Children's Day are in the shape of a fish called carp.

Children's Day is a holiday on 5 May. People fly kites or **streamers** for the children in the family.

The Arts

There are many **traditional crafts** in Japan, such as ink painting, flower arranging, and making beautiful pottery. Origami is the art of making models by folding paper.

Noh theatre has been performed for around 700 years.

Noh is a form of Japanese theatre. Actors wear masks to perform **ancient** stories. Musicians are also on stage and in costume, to **accompany** the actors.

Factfile

Name	Japan is the full name of the country.
Capital	The **capital** of Japan is Tokyo.
Language	Most Japanese speak and write Japanese, but some can also speak Korean and English.
Population	There are about 127 million people living in Japan.
Money	Japanese money is called the yen.
Religions	Most Japanese believe in Buddhism and Shintoism. There are also some Christians.
Products	Japan produces lots of rice, fish, steel, cameras, televisions, radios, ships, cars, chemicals, and toys.

Words you can learn

ichi (ee-tchee)	one
ni (nee)	two
sahn (san)	three
konnichi wa (kon-nee-tchee-wa)	hello
sayonara (sah-yoh-nah-rah)	goodbye
arigato (aree-gah-toh)	thank you
hai (hi)	yes
iie (ee-eh)	no

Glossary

accompany play an instrument while someone else sings or speaks

ancient from a long time ago

capital city where the government is based

character symbol or letter in a writing system

chopsticks a pair of sticks held in one hand to lift food to the mouth

craft skill in making things

drill a safety routine where people practise what to do when there is a danger, like a fire or an earthquake

earthquake violent shaking of the ground

erupt throw out ash and melted rock

respect to value someone or think highly of them

streamer long piece of paper used as decoration

subway trains that run underground through tunnels

traditional the way things have been done or made for a long time

volcano a mountain or hole in the ground that sometimes throws out ash or melted rock from beneath the Earth's surface

Index